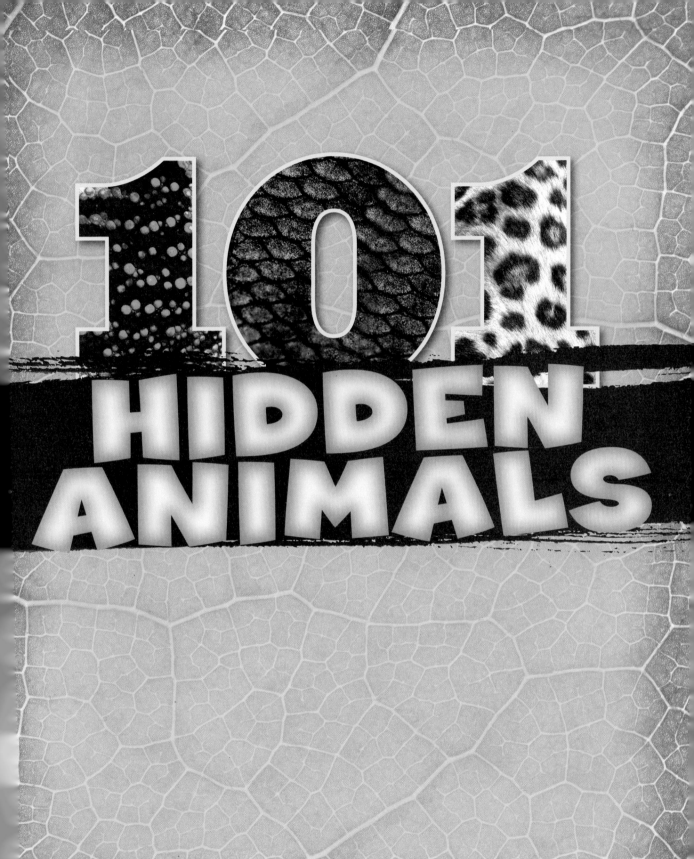

101 HIDDEN ANIMALS

ISBN 978-0-545-67016-6

12 11 10 9 8 7 6 5 4 3 2 1   14 15 16 17 18 19/0

Printed in the U.S.A. 40
First printing, September 2014
Book design by Kay Petronio

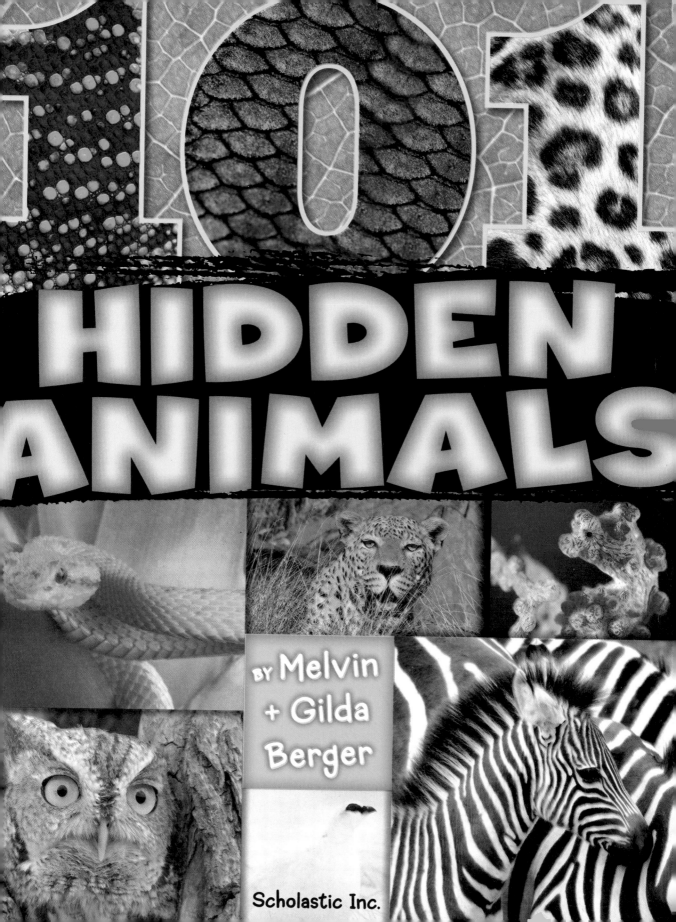

The agama lizard can be green, brown, or gray, and usually lives among rocks or on trees, where it hunts for insects. When threatened by a predator such as a snake or large bird, the agama lizard hides by taking on the colors of its surroundings. When on tree limbs, for example, an agama is the color of bark, but when clinging to boulders, it matches the rocks. Agamas are sometimes called rainbow lizards because the males turn bright red, yellow, and blue during the breeding season.

#1 AGAMA LIZARD: TURNS MANY COLORS

#2 AMBUSH BUG: MASTER OF DISGUISE

Although the ambush bug is a brightly colored insect, it is a master of disguise. Away from its home in the rain forest, the small insect can be seen easily thanks to its brilliant yellow, red, or orange coloring. But when walking among colorful flowers in the forest, the ambush bug is hardly noticeable. To catch its prey, the insect sits motionless and concealed on a flower. Then . . . ZAP! The bug uses its two front legs to grab any passing prey and suck out its body fluids.

The Arctic fox lives in the far north, near the North Pole. In winter, the fox grows a thick, white coat, which keeps it warm amid the ice and snow. This new coat of white fur also makes the Arctic fox nearly invisible, both as predator, sneaking up on lemmings, and as prey, evading polar bears and wolves. In summer months, the fox's fur grows in brown or gray, helping the Arctic fox survive by looking more like the underlying soil and rocks.

#3 ARCTIC FOX: A COAT FOR ALL SEASONS

#4 ARROW CRAB: SKINNY ARMS AND LEGS

At night, an arrow crab hunts for food from its home on the coral reef. By day, it stays hidden and quiet, only becoming active in order to defend its territory from predatory fish. The crab's eight thin legs, two long arms, and pointed head help it blend in with the jagged, surrounding coral. Its skinny, spidery body rarely tempts fish and other predators.

The buff-tip moth is quite common in parks, gardens, and woods throughout Europe. Mainly silver-gray in color, the buff-tip moth has a square head and pale yellow-brown patches at the ends of its wings. During the day, the moth's wings rest against its body, which makes it look like a broken branch. The camouflage fools most predators except bats, which often eat buff-tip moths. Like other moths, the buff-tip moth hunts for food at night.

#5 BUFF-TIP MOTH: LOOKS LIKE A TWIG

6 BULLFROG: HIDES UNDER PLANTS

A greenish back and light-colored belly make excellent camouflage for the bullfrog. But these frogs also have favorite places to hide from predatory snakes, turtles, fish, and birds. Some of the best spots are under tiny plants in the ponds and streams where they live, or among taller plants along the shore. When hungry, the bullfrog usually sits quietly and waits for its prey to come along. This kind of frog is not a picky eater; it will attack any insect, fish, or small mammal that it can swallow.

A butterfly fish appears to have two pairs of eyes! But only one pair is real—the other is camouflage. The true eyes are small and hidden within a dark stripe that runs across the fish's body. The false "eyes" are the much larger black spots on each side of the fish. The stripe and eye spots confuse predators, who can't tell which end of the butterfly fish is the head and which is the tail. Attackers are not able to guess which way the fish will swim to make its escape.

#7 BUTTERFLY FISH: FALSE EYES

#8 CARPET SHARK: RESTS ON THE OCEAN FLOOR

The carpet shark's flat body has many small flaps of skin that make it look like a torn rug on the ocean floor. Its yellow-green or brown skin matches the seaweed-covered rocks that surround it. The fringes of skin that flop around its mouth blur the shape of its head. By day, this powerful predator rests, unmoving and unseen, on a coral reef. At night, it leaves its hiding place and swims over the reef, looking for food. Huge jaws and needlelike teeth allow it to grasp fish and other prey, and gulp them down whole!

Everyone knows that chameleons change color. But few know that the change has more to do with sending messages than matching surroundings! When chameleons turn a different color, they may be sending a signal that they are cold, hot, frightened, angry, or seeking a mate. By constantly changing color they are able to hide very well in the jungles or deserts where they live. Hidden this way, chameleons stand ready to catch insect prey with their super-fast tongues.

#9 CHAMELEON: CHANGES COLORS CONSTANTLY

#10 CHEETAH: HIDES IN TALL GRASSES

The cheetah lives in the grasslands and deserts of Africa. Like many other animals that hunt during daylight, the cheetah must remain hidden in order to locate prey. Its tan-and-black spotted coat blends in with both tall grasses and desert sand, which allows it to ambush impalas, springboks, and hares. So-called tear stripes run from its eyes to the corners of its mouth. Common to many predator animals, these markings shade the cheetah's eyes and help it see while hunting.

The cicada is a chubby, dark-colored insect with four thin, transparent wings that fold like flaps across its body. While male cicadas are known for their noisy "songs," cicadas are hard to see because their color closely matches the trees on which they perch. Cicadas stay underground from four to seventeen years while they grow into adults. Once they emerge, cicadas depend almost entirely on camouflage to protect them from enemy wasps and birds.

#11 CICADA: NOISY, BUT HARD TO SEE

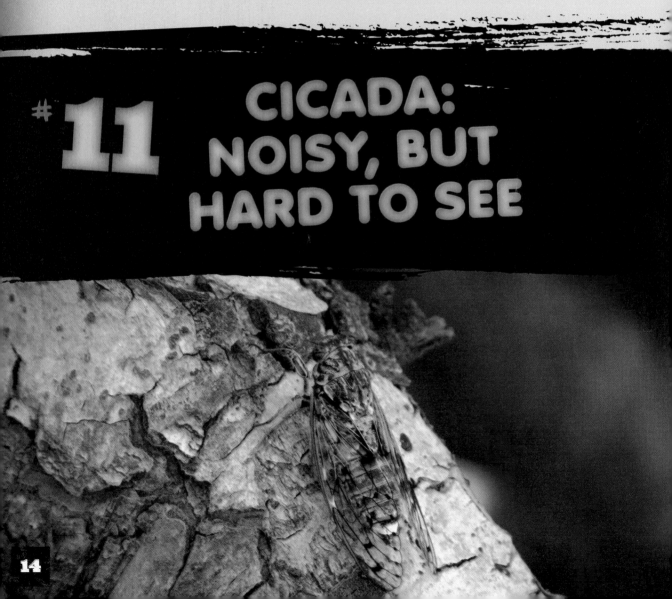

#12 COPPERHEAD SNAKE: PRETTY BUT DEADLY

The entire length of a copperhead's brown body is covered with rusty-red bands that are shaped like hourglasses. This color and pattern give the copperhead amazing cover on the leafy or rocky ground where it slithers. The snake hunts mainly at night for frogs, lizards, and small mammals, which it can kill with one poisonous bite. Young copperheads have a yellow tip on the tail. To attract prey, the snake wiggles its tail. A frog or lizard that comes in for a closer look is quickly snapped up!

Coyotes are rarely seen as they roam across North America's forests, mountains, and prairies. They range in color from light yellow to brownish-red, depending on where they live. Northern coyotes have pale coats, which help them blend in with snow. Coyotes in the West are generally reddish to match their woodland surroundings. Wolves, bears, and other predators often overlook coyotes because they are so well hidden and able to stand very still when frightened.

#13 COYOTE: OUT OF SIGHT

#14 CRAB SPIDER: WATCHES AND WAITS

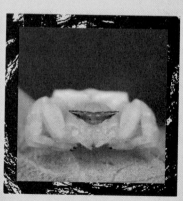

Crab spiders take their name from the way they walk sideways like crabs. These vividly colored insects sit hidden on bright flowers, waiting for their insect prey to appear. Then, at exactly the right moment, they snatch the unsuspecting bugs. Crab spiders can watch and wait on the same plant for days, or even weeks. They can also hide by changing hues to match the flowers on which they perch.

Crocodiles spend their days floating half-hidden in shallow lakes, ponds, swamps, or rivers. Their long, cigar-shaped bodies move along slowly, like big logs floating on water. Only their eyes, ears, and nostrils emerge above the surface, allowing them to see, hear, and breathe. A crocodile's gray-green back and tail merge with the water as it waits to catch any animal that ventures too close. Among its few enemies are jaguars, leopards, anacondas, and pythons.

#15 CROCODILE: FLOATS LIKE A LOG

#16 CUTTLEFISH: QUICK-CHANGE ARTIST

The cuttlefish uses its amazing bag of tricks to hide from enemies, ambush prey, and attract mates. Most incredibly, it can change its skin color, shape, and texture, from smooth to bumpy—all in the blink of an eye! On sand, the cuttlefish looks white or tan. On seaweed, it quickly shifts to a greenish-brown color. Under attack, the cuttlefish can flash lights from its body or squirt brown ink into the water and make a quick getaway.

Decorator crabs, true to their name, dress themselves with objects they find as they crawl along the ocean floor. Seaweed and sponges, pebbles, pieces of coral, and broken seashells stick to the stiff bristles on their backs and legs. Covered with such objects, the crabs look like part of the ocean bottom. Sometimes, plants and animals settle on decorator crabs' bodies and stay there. Enemies then pass them by with hardly a glance.

#17 DECORATOR CRAB: DRESSES IN SEAWEED

18 DEER: FITS IN EASILY

The white-tailed deer is the most common deer in North America. Its color changes with the seasons, which makes it difficult to see the deer in its surroundings. In summer, as it grazes in fields and meadows, a deer's coat is a bright reddish-brown color. In winter, when the deer takes shelter in forests, this color becomes dull and gray. A young deer, or fawn, cannot run fast enough to escape danger. But its brown-and-white spotted fur helps the fawn to hide on the shadowy ground.

The tiny, shy dik-dik spends most of its time hiding among shrubs, bushes, and tall grass in eastern Africa. If a predator approaches, the animal makes a sound through its nose that sounds like "dik-dik," which is how it earned its name. At dawn or dusk, when the light is dim, the dik-dik searches for plants to eat. Mammals such as lions, leopards, hyenas, and cheetahs hunt the dik-dik. When in danger, the dik-dik often starts to flee, but then stops, gets low to the ground, and freezes in place until the danger has passed.

#19 DIK-DIK: HIDES OR FREEZES

#20 DRAGONFLY: LONG, THIN, FAST

A dragonfly's long, slender body may be red, green, or blue, with white, yellow, or black markings. Therefore, the dragonfly can appear at different times to be a twig, leaf, or blade of grass. Predators sometimes look directly at a resting dragonfly but do not see it. In the air, the dragonfly's four large, transparent wings shimmer and gleam in the sunlight. As they dip, dart, and hover, dragonflies easily catch flies and mosquitoes to eat.

On its wings, the emperor moth has two false eyes called eye spots, which look like an owl's eyes. The moth's thin body looks like an owl's beak. Predators see the "eyes" and "beak" and mistake the moth for an owl—too big and frightening to attack. A quick glance at the emperor moth is usually enough to discourage predators.

#21 EMPEROR MOTH: HAS OWL-LIKE EYES

22 FLOUNDER: MATCHES THE SEABED

A flounder is a flat fish that lives at the bottom of the sea and spends most of its life half-buried in soft mud. At birth, the flounder has one eye on each side of its body. But as it grows into an adult, one eye slowly changes position until both are on the same side, looking up! The flounder also changes color and pattern to match the surrounding seabed. Whether resting on the ocean floor or swimming to chase prey, the flounder easily escapes predators' notice.

The lumpy, bumpy, brightly colored frogfish doesn't look like a fish at all. The frogfish has no scales and uses its fins for walking rather than for swimming. In fact, the frogfish most closely resembles a multicolored rock on the ocean floor. Sometimes a careless fish or crab swims too near. Pop! The frogfish flings open its huge mouth. Water rushes in, carrying with it the unlucky prey,

#23 FROGFISH: STONY AND FLASHY

#24 GABOON VIPER: FOREST FLOOR DISGUISE

Gaboon vipers live on the floor of tropical rain forests, where the ground is covered with dead leaves and broken branches. The snake's brown, beige, white, and black patterned skin blends right in with the leafy litter that blankets the earth. Since rain forest trees block most of the sun's rays, little light reaches the forest floor. Here, the viper is almost invisible. Monkeys and other prey often fail to see the Gaboon viper—and its huge mouth—until it's too late!

A genet is a gray mammal with small, dark spots on its body, and a long, striped, bushy tail. The genet lives in a variety of habitats across Europe and Africa, including deserts, forests, and grasslands. It hunts at night by crouching low and moving forward slowly. Then it pounces on its prey! During the day, the sleeping genet is concealed by spots and stripes. The markings help it blend into the background, hiding it from predatory owls, snakes, and leopards.

#25 GENET: SPOTS AND STRIPES

26 GHOST CRAB: VANISHES FROM SIGHT

The ghost crab spends much of its time in a deep burrow that it digs in the sand of an ocean beach. The crab's underground home protects it from the intense heat of the sun. But when foraging for food aboveground, it must avoid predators such as raccoons and large shorebirds. When the crab senses danger, it flattens its body and buries itself in a shallow hole under the sand. It also changes color to blend in with the light brown sand. Not surprisingly, the ghost crab got its name because of the way it vanishes from sight.

The ghost mantis is extremely small and brown, sometimes mixed with green. Tiny irregular flaps of flesh stick out from its legs and wings, mimicking leaves with chewed-off edges. To hide its body and confuse predators, the ghost mantis changes shape by tucking its front legs up against its body. Sometimes it sways gently back and forth, like a leaf blowing in the breeze. When hunting, the ghost mantis hangs from a branch, looking more like a shriveled leaf than a predator.

#27 GHOST MANTIS: BLOWIN' IN THE WIND

#28 GHOST PIPEFISH: ABOUT THE SIZE OF YOUR FINGER!

Predators are rarely able to catch the ghost pipefish, even though it lives in shallow water around coastal ocean reefs. First of all, the ghost pipefish is very small, not much longer than the index finger on your hand. Second, the fish is camouflaged by short, thin, fleshy threads that completely cover its branch-like body. When feeding, the ghost pipefish disappears into the seaweed and coral, making it hard to spot.

A giant swallowtail caterpillar does not defend itself by hiding. Instead, it takes on the color and shape of bird droppings! When attacked by enemy ants or spiders, the caterpillar also emits a terrible smell, like stinky cat litter. If neither of these defenses works, the caterpillar may rear up and wave its two long, red horns. To be sure, this often does the trick. Most predators will look elsewhere for their next meal.

#29 GIANT SWALLOWTAIL CATERPILLAR: LOOKS LIKE BIRD DROPPINGS

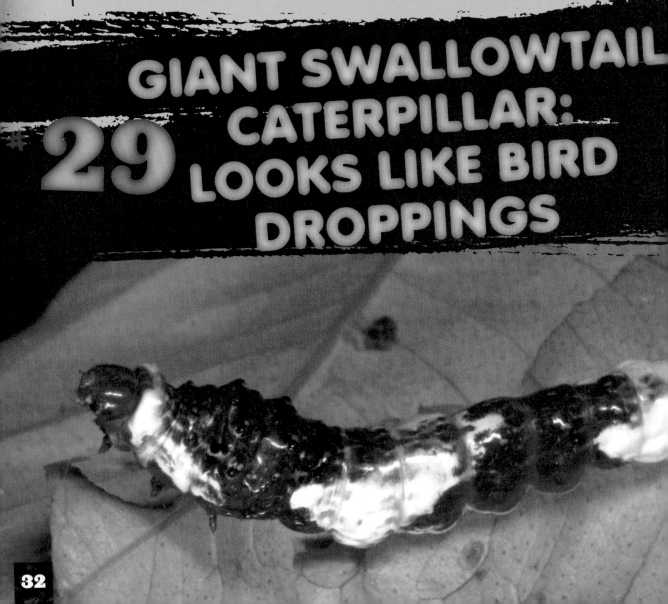

#30 GIRAFFE: MERGES WITH THE TREES

Giraffes roam among the tall trees and on the open plains of Africa. Each giraffe has a unique pattern of light brown patches separated by thick, white lines. Like cracks on an old plate, the lines break up the surface of the giraffe's body and hide its true size and shape. In sunlight and shadow, a giraffe's coat is difficult to tell apart from the trees. Adult giraffes blend in so well with the trees that they are rarely surprised by lions, their most feared predators.

The amazing freshwater glass catfish is almost as transparent as a clear pane of glass. Unlike most fish, it has no scales. Only the slightly darker head, bones, and organs are visible to the naked eye. The glass catfish swims in large Asian rivers, usually near the shore, where it hides from predators by swimming among thickly growing plants. Feelers protrude on either side of its mouth to help it locate water bugs, small fish, and other food.

#31 GLASS CATFISH: TOTALLY TRANSPARENT

#32 GLASSWING BUTTERFLY: OUT-OF-SIGHT WINGS

The glasswing butterfly is protected by four transparent wings. Each wing is bordered in brown, with only a patch of white near the top. When the butterfly lands on a flower, light passes right through the wings and its body fades into the background. A predator hunting for food is able to see only the flower, not the insect. When in flight, all that is visible is a bobbing white spot, and so the butterfly remains safe.

Gray tree frogs are born in ponds or lakes, but spend most of their time perched high above in trees. Their splotchy, gray-and-black bodies look just like rough tree bark! However, sometimes gray tree frogs change color and become light green. Scientists are unsure whether they do this to help them hide better, or to adjust to changes in temperature or humidity. Whatever the reason, the different color improves their already excellent camouflage.

33 GRAY TREE FROG: CLEVER COLOR CHANGE

34 GREAT BITTERN: STANDS STILL AS A STATUE

To hide itself, the great bittern assumes a "camouflage posture." The bird stands frozen in place, with bill pointing straight up and neck stretched out. The great bittern's pale-brown speckled plumage helps it disappear amid the reedy marshes it calls home. The great bittern is so well camouflaged that its enemies—from owls to house cats—can't even see it up close.

During the day, the great potoo sleeps, perched upright on a branch or tree stump. The bird's eyes are closed, but small holes, like peepholes, allow it to see. Its speckled, gray-and-brown feathers blend in perfectly with the tree in which it sits. Monkeys, falcons, and other predators often cannot tell where the tree ends and the potoo begins. At night, the potoo hunts for flying insects, birds, and bats with its bright, yellow-orange eyes wide open.

#35 GREAT POTOO: EYELIDS WITH PEEPHOLES

#36 HARP SEAL: PUPS ON ICE

The body of the harp seal is dark on top with a light belly. When seen from above, the seal's dark back blends in with the water. From below, the white underside merges with the light sky. A young harp seal, however, is born with all-white fur. The white color conceals the helpless pup on the ice or snow, making it harder to be seen by an enemy polar bear. After about a month, when the pup can care for itself, its fur slowly darkens to that of an adult harp seal.

Long-legged herons can hide by standing as still as statues. They take cover among the tall plants that grow near ponds, streams, marshes, and swamps. From its upright position, a heron is good at spotting fish and other prey, such as frogs and snakes. Then it moves its head from side to side as if to judge the animal's exact position. Lightning fast, the heron stabs the prey with its long, sharp bill and devours it.

#37 HERON: HIDES, THEN STRIKES

38 HONEYBEE: YELLOW MEANS DANGER!

The colorful black-and yellow honeybee spends most of its time flitting from flower to flower. When atop a yellow sunflower, the bee is well camouflaged. But black and yellow are warning colors in nature. On a flower of any other hue, the bee's colors scare enemies away. Bears, birds, and skunks, their worst enemies, remember that bees have a nasty sting. Predators will often flee rather than risk being stung by a honeybee.

Horned lizards usually live in a dry, sandy environment and bask in the sun to stay warm. Their reddish-brown color looks like the desert floor and helps them blend in with their habitat. Pointed spines along their sides blur the lizard's shape. Very long spines form a so-called crown of horns and add to the disguise. When threatened or frightened, the horned lizard spreads itself flat on the ground, casting no shadows that might give it away.

#39 HORNED LIZARD: CROWN OF HORNS

#40 HORNED VIPER: COLOR OF SAND

The horned viper snake has a sand-colored body that blends in well with its natural habitat, the Sahara and other dry, sandy deserts. To hide even more effectively, the snake wiggles into the sand, and hides with only its horns, eyes, and nose showing above the surface. Scientists say that the viper has two special scales that look like little "horns," which they believe either improve the camouflage or protect its eyes from the sand.

The impala is a mammal that resembles a deer or antelope. It lives around the edges of Africa's grasslands and woodlands. Here it finds good places to hide among low tree branches, tall grass, and large bushes. The impala is dark on its top and sides, and light on the belly and tail, which makes it hard to spot in sunlight. Sun and shadows even out the color of the impala, adding to the disguise.

#41 IMPALA: GOOD HIDING PLACES

42 LEAF INSECT: WALKING LEAF

The slender leaf insect has the flat shape and green color of an old, withered leaf. Ragged edges on its large wings look like bite marks. Some are so well camouflaged that other leaf insects bite them by mistake! When a leaf insect walks, it sways gently, like a leaf in a breeze—a "walking" leaf. The leaf insect lives in tropical forests and spends its days sitting motionless among the leaves. At night, the leaf insect emerges and looks for leaves to eat.

Katydids are green or brown insects with large wings. They feed on trees and bushes with leaves that almost exactly match the katydids' size, color, and shape. Moreover, these insects also have veins on their wings and position themselves at the same angle as the growing leaves. They are so well hidden that predator birds and monkeys often have trouble finding them. For some reason, only the praying mantis seems able to hunt them down.

#43 LEAF KATYDID: HIDDEN IN TREES

#44 LEAF-TAILED GECKO: DISAPPEARING ACT

Leaf-tailed geckos make their home in the rain forests of Madagascar, where they spend their days resting flat and facedown against a tree limb. Their bumpy skin is a mottled mixture of brown, gray, tan, and black. Some leaf-tailed geckos resemble lichen, and others look more like the bark of a tree. A leaf-tailed gecko hides itself so well that a predator owl, eagle, rat, or snake can come very close without knowing it's there.

The leafy sea dragon lives along ocean coasts and usually surrounds itself with thick beds of seaweed and sea grass. Instead of scales, the leafy sea dragon is covered with layers of hard, bony plates. Protruding from these plates are growths that resemble leaves, making it nearly impossible to detect among the sea plants. Large fish are fooled by the way the sea dragon slowly sways back and forth, like seaweed in flowing water.

45 LEAFY SEA DRAGON: SEAWEED LOOK-ALIKE

46 LEOPARD: WATCH OUT ABOVE!

The leopard, smallest of all big cats, has a tan coat covered with black, rose-shaped spots called rosettes. The exact shade of tan depends on where it lives—lighter in grasslands and darker in forests. When hunting on land, leopards crouch low and silently stalk their prey. They are shielded by the thick undergrowth of tall grass and bushes. Leopards are also climbers that hunt from trees. Here they sit, unseen among the leaves, waiting to pounce on passing prey.

The lichen spider usually hides on the bark of a tree that is covered with—you guessed it!—lichen. Instead of building a web, the large spider sits on the tree, frozen in place. Its striped and speckled surface creates a camouflage that hides the insect from sight. Hairs and bumps on its long legs obscure the edges of its body and enhance the illusion. When a hapless bug comes along, the spider springs into action and uses its powerful legs to overcome its prey.

#47 LICHEN SPIDER: AMBUSHES PREY

#48 LION: PREDATOR IN THE GRASS

Lions have short coats of light brown fur, which blend perfectly with the dry grasses of the African plains. Lions often hunt at night because they are harder to see in dim light. This allows them to hide and stalk prey such as zebras, gazelles, and giraffes. To surprise its victim, the lion moves slowly, its body close to the ground. Then the lion leaps and swiftly makes a kill by breaking the victim's neck or biting its throat.

In the coral reef, there are hardly any fish more unusual than the lionfish. Dazzling red and white stripes obscure the lionfish's size and shape. They also warn enemies away. An even better defense is the lionfish's needle-shaped spines that deliver fatal doses of poison. A hunting lionfish uses its spines to steer small fish against the coral reef. Then it injects them with poison and slurps them down.

#49 LIONFISH: SPINES OF POISON

50 LONGNOSE HAWKFISH: WATCH OUT FOR THE SNOUT

Predators have a hard time finding the longnose hawkfish among the clumps of thin coral on tropical reefs. The fish's body is crisscrossed with red and white stripes and resembles strands of coral. Like a bird of prey, the hawkfish perches unmoving on the reef, scouting for activity of any nearby small fish or shrimp. Then, in a flash, the longnose hawkfish darts out and sucks up dinner through its long snout.

The looper moth caterpillar earned its name from the way it "loops" along, inch by inch. Thin, wavy lines on its green or brown body make the caterpillar resemble a bump on a leaf or plant. But, when in danger, the looper moth caterpillar stands straight up. Suddenly, it more closely resembles a twig than a caterpillar. Bump or twig, it doesn't look like anything that predatory birds would consider eating.

#51 LOOPER MOTH CATERPILLAR: STANDS UP STRAIGHT

52 MARSUPIAL FROG: BLENDS INTO THE FOREST FLOOR

Marsupial frogs live in the rain forests of South America and on the slopes of the Andes mountains. Their patchy, light-brown skin looks like the leaves that cover the ground. The little frogs depend on their color to hide from snakes, large birds, and certain mammals. Safely hidden, the hungry marsupial frogs wait on the leafy cover for the bugs to come near them. At just the right moment, the frog snaps up its prey!

The skin of the mossy frog is covered in bumps and is mostly brown, speckled with green. Small growths and spines stick out from the frog's body so that it looks like it is covered with clumps of moss. When hiding under a rock or floating plant in the water, the mossy frog is invisible to its enemies. When frightened and unable to hide, the little frog folds itself into a ball and plays dead!

#53 MOSSY FROG: SKIN LIKE CLUMPY MOSS

#54 NEEDLE SHRIMP: COPYCAT CORAL

The needle shrimp was named for its long, thin body and sharply pointed head. This little creature keeps out of sight in the water by perching on coral or grass. Thousands of shrimp can cluster on coral or sea grass without even one separating from the rest. While swimming, the needle shrimp moves sideways, like a piece of drifting seaweed.

Nighthawks are birds speckled with brown, gray, and white feathers that provide them with great cover. It helps the birds vanish in the dim light of evening, night, and early dawn, when they are most active. This camouflage protects them from attack by predators such as skunks, foxes, crows, and ravens. During the day, most night-flying birds sleep perched **across** tree limbs. But not the nighthawks. They perch **along** tree limbs, for safety's sake.

#55 NIGHTHAWK: PERCHES ALONG TREE LIMBS

#56 NIGHTJAR: A LEAFY LIFE

Nightjars' feathers are a mass of gray, brown, and white patches and stripes. This coloring breaks up their shape and also causes them to resemble dead leaves or tree bark, in order to fool enemies. Multicolored feathers help them hide in their nests, which they build in leaf litter on the ground. These feathers also hide nightjars when they roost on tree limbs. At dawn or dusk, nightjars hunt and catch flying insects that can neither see nor hear their attackers.

When chased by a bird, the oak leaf butterfly may suddenly land and lift its wings. Now, only the dark undersides of its wings are visible, and the butterfly looks more like a dead leaf than a colorful insect! It remains hidden for as long as it holds its wings together. But after danger passes, the butterfly spreads open its wings to reveal bands of orange on a light blue-and-black background—and it looks just like another flower.

#57 OAK LEAF BUTTERFLY: UPRIGHT WINGS

58 OCTOPUS: PLAYS TRICKS

Few animals have as many ways to hide and escape from predators as an octopus. When frightened, it changes color and pattern, and disappears into almost any undersea environment. It can flatten its body and squeeze through narrow openings between rocks where larger creatures cannot follow. If pursued, the octopus squirts a blob of ink into the water that blocks the enemy's view. Then it just swims away!

The orchid mantis is a beautiful white-and-pink insect with six amazing legs that look like flower petals. The mantis spends its life sitting perfectly still on white-and-pink orchids that grow in South Asia. It waits patiently for smaller insects to land on the flowers to gather pollen. Often, the insects do not spot the camouflaged mantis until it grabs them with its two front legs. Lizards, toads, and other predators, also frequently miss the hidden mantis.

#59 ORCHID MANTIS: MARVELOUS LEGS

#60 OWL: FLUFFY FEATHERS

Many owls hide in big, old trees during the day. Long, fluffy, dull-brown feathers let them blend in with the bark. The birds hunt for food after dark, and even then depend on their plumage to conceal them. The feathers make the birds seem larger than they actually are, further confusing predators and prey. The owls' beating wings make no sound as they swoop down to snatch up mice, rats, chipmunks, or squirrels!

A pair of male and female oystercatchers build a nest in which to hide their eggs. First they scrape a shallow nest into the rocky ground. Then they use their long beaks to flip rocks, pebbles, and broken shells into the nest. The nest now looks much like the surrounding ground. When it's ready, the female lays about three gray, speckled eggs inside. The eggs look so much like the rocks that predators cannot tell which is which.

#61 OYSTERCATCHER: DISGUISED EGGS

62 PANTHER: STEALTHY HUNTER

The term panther can refer to any large leopard, cougar, mountain lion, or puma with a sleek, black fur coat. Shiny black fur is the perfect cover for these cautious nighttime hunters that move silently through the rain forests of Asia and Africa seeking prey. But panthers are also good climbers. By day, they rest high in the trees, hidden from dangerous enemies by the dense foliage.

Many parrots are adorned with feathers of striking color, which are surprisingly good camouflage in their tropical habitat. The birds virtually disappear in the shadows cast by the bright sun on the colorful trees and flowers. The camouflage also protects parrots from predators such as other large birds, snakes, and monkeys, as well as from humans who capture them for food, feathers, or as pets.

#63 PARROT: BOLD COLORS

#64 PARTRIDGE: HIDES ON THE FARM

Grayish-brown partridges hide on farms or in open grasslands, where they use tall plants for cover. Here they also find wheat, corn, rye, and green leafy plants to feed on. Partridges are very fast creatures, often preferring to escape danger by running rather than flying. Unfortunately, they are also favorite game birds for human hunters. Hunters use dogs to locate the well-hidden partridges and force them from their shelters.

The peppered moth needs all the help it can get to avoid predators, especially birds. The moth's main line of defense is the black-and-white dotted pattern on its wings. In order to blend in, the moth usually lands on tree bark or rocks that match its wing pattern. And to make it even harder to see, the peppered moth often rests by day in the shadow of a branch, or on a leafy twig. Altogether, its camouflage is hard to beat!

#65 PEPPERED MOTH: SPECKLED WINGS

66 PHEASANT: BLENDS INTO SHADOWS

Pheasants make their homes in places with natural cover in which to hide. Grassy fields, farmlands, or woodlands with thick growths of shrubs and trees are where most pheasants live. Enemies, such as foxes, coyotes, owls, hawks, and even human hunters, find pheasants hard to spot in the wild. Their speckled, multicolored feathers blend right in with the shady light of the woods. The shadowy foliage also conceals the ground hollows where pheasants build nests.

A pika is a small, furry plant-eater much like a mouse that lives high on cool mountain slopes. Its thick, gray, long-haired coat blends in with the rocks and keeps it warm in the winter. During the summer, the pika's coat thins out for the warm weather and becomes brown. This color helps the pika hide in the grass, weeds, and wildflowers of its habitat. When frightened, a pika emits a short, high-pitched "eek!" to warn predators away.

#67 PIKA: CHANGES ITS COAT

#68 POISON DART FROG: BRIGHT WARNING COLORS

Poison dart frogs are boldly colored animals that do not try to hide or blend in like other types of frogs. Instead, they attract attention with striking coloration: yellow, gold, red, green, blue, black. The colors warn other animals—and humans, too—to leave the frogs alone. Like other animals with warning colors, these frogs are very poisonous. Once a predator bites or even touches a poison dart frog, it becomes very sick and stays away forever.

Polar bears have a special kind of fur that hides them in their icy habitat. Each hair is actually hollow and colorless, but light reflected from the ice and snow make the fur look white. Often, the polar bears' dark eyes and nose are the only parts of their body that can readily be seen. That's why a polar bear sometimes covers its face with its paws while waiting to catch ringed seals, its favorite prey, when they come up for air.

#69 POLAR BEAR: COAT OF HOLLOW HAIRS!

#70 PRAYING MANTIS: WAITS AND GRABS

The praying mantis is found throughout the world, either on plants or in grass. Its green or brown color matches the grass and twigs where it lives. Mostly, it sits patiently in one place waiting for moths or grasshoppers to come along. Then it grabs and holds the prey with its two front legs. The camouflage provides good protection from bat, bird, and spider foes. If threatened, the praying mantis is known to rear up and bite its attacker.

The ptarmigan bird lives in cold, northern lands and has feathers that change color depending upon the season. In winter, its feathers are white, like snow. The birds hide in the snowy banks where eagles and Arctic foxes cannot find them. In summer, when the snow melts and plants sprout, the ptarmigan grows new feathers that are gray and speckled brown. Now the ptarmigan blends into the ground as it seeks berries and other foods to eat.

#71 PTARMIGAN: CHANGES COLOR WITH THE SEASON

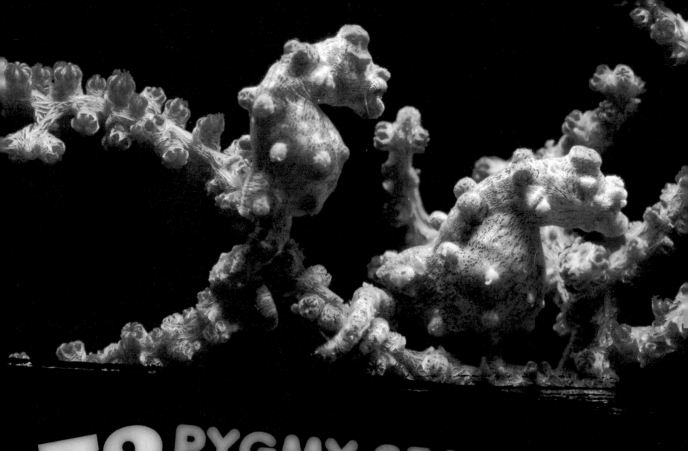

#72 PYGMY SEAHORSE: HIDES IN CORAL

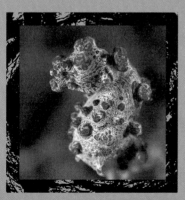

The pygmy seahorse is almost too small to see—about the size of a paper clip. Its surface is gray or purple with pink or red bumps, which seamlessly matches the coral around which it floats. Because of the way it looks in the water, very few predator fish recognize the pygmy seahorse as a tasty morsel. In fact, its camouflage works so well that scientists did not even know the fish existed until 1969!

A rattlesnake usually lurks on the ground, among rocks or fallen leaves. There it waits to attack its prey. As soon as a rabbit or other prey approaches, the snake lunges and bites. The rattlesnake depends on its drab, patterned skin for disguise. When a predator comes along, the frightened snake shakes the dry rings at the tip of its tail. This makes a buzzing noise that warns the predator away and lets the snake escape.

#73 RATTLESNAKE: PLAYS HIDE-AND-SEEK

#74 SAND CRAB: BURIED UP TO THE EYES

A sand crab spends most of its time on an ocean beach among the breaking waves. The only body parts that remain above the sand are two eyestalks and two antennae for capturing food from the rushing water. The sand crab gets extra camouflage from its gray or sand-colored shell. Well concealed, the crab keeps quite safe from predatory fish and birds. Five pairs of legs let the sand crab swim, crawl, walk, and dig quickly—but always backward.

Most scorpion fish are a dull mixture of gray and brown. They are covered with warts, spots, ridges, grooves, and hanging flaps of skin. Their predators, which include sharks, rays, and eels, can rarely tell them apart from the debris on the ocean floor. From near or far, the fish look like pieces of coral, or rocks covered with sand. Scorpion fish hide in reefs or rocks by day. At night they quietly lie in one place, ready and waiting to snap up tasty passersby.

#75 SCORPION FISH: INVISIBLE ON THE OCEAN FLOOR

#76 SEAHORSE: PRESTO CHANGE-O

Since the seahorse is a slow swimmer with little ability to defend itself, it depends entirely on its color and shape for protection. In just a few minutes, this fish can change color and pattern to match its surroundings. By growing short threads of extra skin, the seahorse suddenly looks more like sea grass or coral than a living animal. Sometimes tiny plants grow on the seahorse's hard, stony body, which help hide it even better in the water.

The sidewinder is a poisonous snake that lives in the Namib desert in Africa. To hide from predators and prey, the sidewinder often burrows well below the hot surface, where the sand is cooler. In less than twenty seconds, a sidewinder can wiggle into its hiding place. Because it has poor hearing, it cannot always hear danger approach. But with eyes on top of its head, the sidewinder can watch above the sand, even while most of its body is buried below.

#77 SIDEWINDER: SLITHERS IN SAND

78 SLOTH: A FURRY GREEN COAT

The sloth spends its time in the rain forest trees of Central and South America. The animal moves so slowly that algae grows on its furry coat. This gives the sloth's thick, grayish-brown fur a greenish tint, which makes the animal hard to see as it hangs from branches by its long claws. A sloth easily escapes notice, too, because it sleeps upside down for up to eighteen hours a day. Some even rest at the top of palm trees, where they look like coconuts!

The smooth green snake is the color of the grass in North American meadows where it is most at home. The snake blends in so perfectl[y] that its prey—crickets, grasshoppers, and caterpillars—usually don't even see it coming. When in danger, the smooth green snake slips a short distance away, "stands," and then sways gently, like a plant blowing in the breeze. Their color and swaying save many smooth green snakes from being eaten by enemy hawks and raccoons.

#79 SMOOTH GREEN SNAKE: SWAYS LIKE GRASS IN THE BREEZE

#80 SNAPPING TURTLE: HIDES IN MUDDY WATER

A snapping turtle is dark brown, green, or near-black—the colors of the sluggish lakes, ponds, rivers, or streams in which it lives. To catch its prey, the hungry snapping turtle buries itself among the plants or mud, with only its head at the surface. The turtle is still, except for its bright red tongue, which wiggles like a worm. As fish, frogs, snakes, or small animals try to catch the "worm," the snapping turtle moves lightning fast to snatch and swallow its meal.

The gray, spotted snow leopard lives in the cold mountain ranges of central Asia. Its long, thick fur hides this predator against the sharp rocks of its mountain home, and also keeps it warm. The spots grow paler in winter, and the snow leopard becomes nearly invisible in its frigid habitat. In fact, it is so well concealed that it's sometimes called the ghost of the Himalayas. Unnoticed, the snow leopard stalks its prey, then takes a giant leap to nab a wild sheep or deer.

#81 SNOW LEOPARD: LURKS AMONG THE ROCKS

#82 SNOWSHOE HARE: A WHITE COAT FOR WINTER

Snowshoe hares live in the coldest regions of the northern United States and Canada. In winter, most of these hares grow white coats so they cannot be seen against the snow. Sometimes they dig shallow burrows for shelter and to stay out of sight. With the melting snow of spring, the hares' coats slowly turn gray-brown to match the ground. With a new coat, snowshoe hares avoid foxes, lynxes, and coyotes—their worst enemies.

The snowy owl is very well camouflaged for life in the Arctic. It has a round face, with tufts of hair around its head. Its face, legs, and feet are covered with thin, white, fur-like feathers. The owl's body is usually white with dark spots or bands running from side to side. Adults hide from view until they spot and snatch an animal with their strong, sharp claws. These birds fear few predators, except for wolves and Arctic foxes, which they dive-bomb to scare away.

#83 SNOWY OWL: COVERED WITH WHITE FEATHERS

#84 SPOTTED THICK-KNEE: KNOBBY KNEES GIVE IT AWAY

The spotted thick-knee is a common bird in Africa that has spotted gray or brown feathers. The bird hides itself so well that it is seldom seen in the woodlands, country fields, and city parks where it lives. The bird must take care because it does have thick knees on bright yellow legs, which can sometimes betray its location. A spotted thick-knee may be attacked by eagles or owls while guarding the nest. Then, the thick-knee pretends to have a broken wing in order to distract its predator.

The spring peeper's tan-and-brown coloring makes it nearly invisible on trees, rocks, or the ground. When standing motionless, a peeper looks more like tree bark or ground litter than a little frog. To further camouflage itself, the spring peeper can also darken or lighten its skin color. It seeks food at night, when the light is too dim for snakes and birds to hunt it down. The peeper's loud call makes it easier to hear than to see!

#85 SPRING PEEPER: PEEPS APLENTY

#86 SQUID: AN INKY ESCAPE

A squid is similar to an octopus, except that it has two long tentacles in addition to its eight arms. It also has a sack of ink in its body that it uses as protection. When threatened, the squid contracts its muscles and squirts out ink, clouding the water and confusing its attacker. Then, the fleeing squid emits a jet of water to spread the ink around. And, like the octopus, the squid can change colors to blend into its background—as often as a thousand times a day!

The stargazer fish doesn't actually watch stars. In fact, most of the time, it hides on the sandy bottom of the sea. Its dusty-white skin is almost the same color as the sand. Only the stargazer's eyes and upturned mouth protrude from the ocean floor. From this hiding place, the stargazer sits and waits for unsuspecting prey to swim by. Some stargazers have a lure that hangs from its mouth. To certain fish, the lure looks like something to eat. If a fish swims toward the "bait," the stargazer snaps it up.

#87 STARGAZER: A SANDY HOME ON THE OCEAN FLOOR

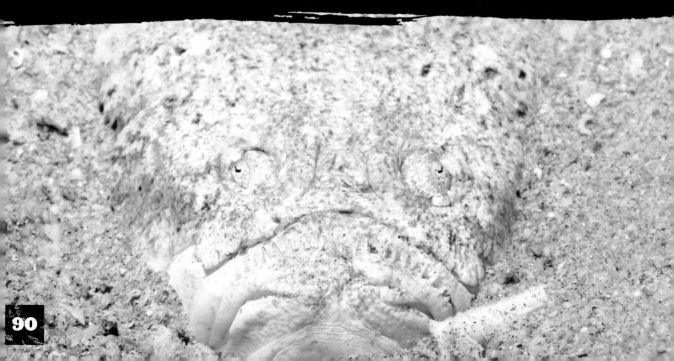

#88 STICK INSECT: TWIGS ON LEGS

With their long, thin bodies and legs, stick insects can be mistaken for twigs or stalks of grass. Usually green or brown in color, none look like tempting insect snacks. These tropical bugs spend most of their days in one spot, usually without stirring. Sometimes, they trick enemies by falling down and playing dead. At dusk, when bird and lizard predators sleep, the stick insects get busy. They walk about, looking for leaves to eat, swaying gently back and forth in the breeze.

A stingray is a large, flat fish that lives in shallow ocean waters. Tan-colored skin flecked with blue blends right into its watery home. It swims along, propelling itself with wide, flapping, wavelike fins. When hunting for prey, a stingray settles down on the seafloor and lightly covers itself with sand. There it sits, waiting for passing prey such as crabs, fish, and mussels. Even excellent hunters like sharks and orcas can overlook it and swim right past.

#89 STINGRAY: MOVES LIKE AN OCEAN WAVE

90 STONE GRASSHOPPER: MISTAKEN IDENTITY

The squat stone grasshopper lives mostly on dry, rocky plains where few plants or flowers grow. Among the stones and shadows, this grasshopper can be easily mistaken for another pebble on the ground. Its wings are tiny and it does not use them for flying. A grasshopper hops! Although well camouflaged, the stone grasshopper is still vulnerable to attack. In defense, the grasshopper kicks out its long, powerful hind legs and emits a loud, raspy, warning sound.

Stonefish are mottled in color, with remarkably bumpy and knobby skin. When a stonefish comes to rest on the ocean floor, it closely resembles a rock or piece of coral. Here the fish sits motionless and is very difficult for predators to detect. The stonefish has thirteen very sharp spines, each with two poisonous glands at the base. When touched, the spines pop up and inject victims with a deadly dose of poison.

#91 STONEFISH: ROCK, CORAL, OR FISH?

#92 STRIPED BURROWING FROG: LIKE A BLADE OF GRASS

The striped burrowing frog is impressively disguised by a bright, greenish-yellow streak down its back. The frog looks more like blades of grass, and not like a frog at all. Given its blotchy brown, olive, and green skin, the frog also blends in with leaves, twigs, and other matter on the ground or in the water. The striped burrowing frog is native to Australia, where it hops around ponds and pools near people's homes. Small wonder that one of its primary predators is the house cat!

The oddly shaped Surinam toad has a flat body and triangular head. It spends its entire life lying in the water at the bottom of ponds and swamps in South America, resembling a waterlogged leaf or rock. The dark spots on its rough brown skin look just like shadows on the water. The Surinam toad waits to ambush its prey and uses its long, thin fingers to push worms, insects, shellfish, and fish into its mouth.

#93 SURINAM TOAD: A LEAF . . . WITH LEGS?!

#94 TAPIR: SPECKLED AND SPOTTED BABY

The adult tapir is a huge, powerful animal that fears few predators. However, the baby tapir is vulnerable as it waits alone for its mother to return from gathering food. Fortunately, the baby's coat has a display of streaks and spots that help conceal it in the shade of tall, tropical trees overhead. Predators often completely overlook the baby tapir. After about six months, the young one is better able to defend itself, and the camouflage fades.

During the day, the tawny frogmouth bird sits on a tree limb, upright and unmoving. With its head tilted up and eyes closed in slits, it looks like a broken tree limb. The tawny frogmouth's mottled gray-and-brown feathers are a perfect match for the tree's bark. However, if an enemy sees through this disguise, the tawny frogmouth fluffs out its feathers, shows its bright, orange eyes, and opens its frog-like mouth to reveal a startling, yellow throat.

#95 TAWNY FROGMOUTH: FULL OF SURPRISES

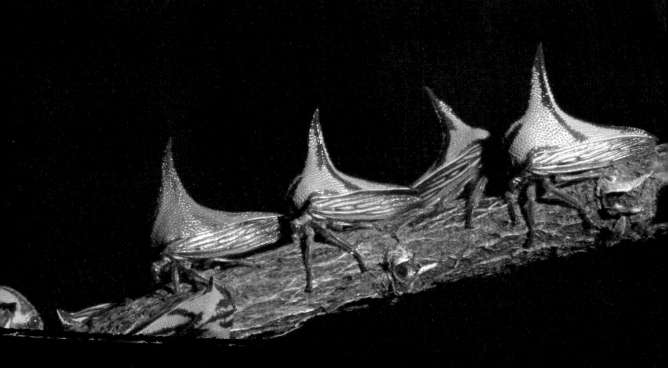

#96 THORN BUG: COMES TO A POINT

The thorn bug's hard, outer shell makes the animal as short and sharp as a thorn on a rosebush. And just as a thorn protects a plant, the shell protects the bug. The thorn bug can usually avoid danger by crawling away from its attacker. Occasionally, a bird or other predator gets near enough to attack. Not only does the bug's "thorn" deliver a painful wound, but its body tastes dreadful. One bite is usually enough to keep the enemy away forever.

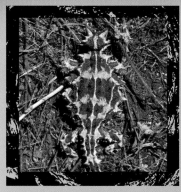

Although the thorny devil is a timid, friendly little lizard, its appearance is quite frightening. Covered in many bumps and lumps, its exact size and shape are quite difficult to make out. Pointy horns on its head and spikes on its body hide it on the rocks, sand, or dry plants of central Australia. When in danger, the lizard dips its head between its front legs, revealing the clump on its back that suddenly resembles a second head. Then even buzzards flee!

#97 THORNY DEVIL: TWO HEADS ARE BETTER THAN ONE

98 TIGER: STRIPED AND FEROCIOUS

Most tigers are orange with black stripes. But no two have exactly the same pattern of stripes, just as no two humans have the same fingerprints. The dark stripes give tigers excellent camouflage as they wait for prey among tall grasses and brush. Tigers hunt at night in the forests and grasslands across Asia where most of them live. Once the buffalo, deer, pig, or other prey is spotted, a tiger creeps silently forward. When close, it pounces at lightning speed to kill its victim.

Most turacos are green-colored birds with long tails that live in the treetops of African forests. Since they are poor, clumsy flyers that cannot quickly escape their enemies, turacos depend on their greenish plumage to hide them amid the leaves. When in danger, a turaco sits as still as a statue until the predator draws close. Then, suddenly, it spreads its giant wings, revealing a shocking patch of brilliant red. That usually works! The red patch startles the enemy and also warns any other turacos away.

#99 TURACO: A RED SURPRISE

#100 WOOLLY APHID: COTTON CANDY CAMOUFLAGE

Woolly aphids are insects that feed on plant juices and secrete a sticky, sugary waste called honeydew. It flows in long, thin streams that look like cotton candy, and covers the insect, giving it a fluffy appearance. Although easy to see, the honeydew protects woolly aphids from predators. The aphids' white covering looks like mold, which almost no animal wants to eat! When feeding together, woolly aphids often form large cottony masses, which also discourage attackers.

Zebras are known for their dashing pattern of black and white stripes. When one zebra stands alone on the African grassland, its stripes are quite obvious. But a single zebra is seldom seen in the wild. Zebras are social animals that live and move in herds. As a group, their stripes create a stunning—but confusing—effect. Lions, the zebras' chief predators, find it almost impossible to separate one zebra from the herd, and will often give up the hunt.

#101 ZEBRA: HEADS OR TAILS

INDEX

PHOTO CREDITS

101
FREAKY ANIMALS

BY Melvin + Gilda Berger

SCHOLASTIC

101
ANIMAL babies

BY Melvin + Gilda Berger

SCHOLASTIC

ABOUT THE AUTHORS

MELVIN AND GILDA BERGER are the authors of more than two hundred books for children. Their books have received awards from the National Science Teachers Association, the Library of Congress, and the New York Public Library. The Bergers live in New York.

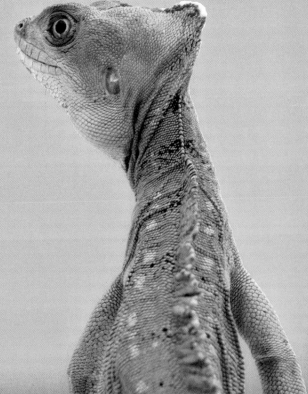